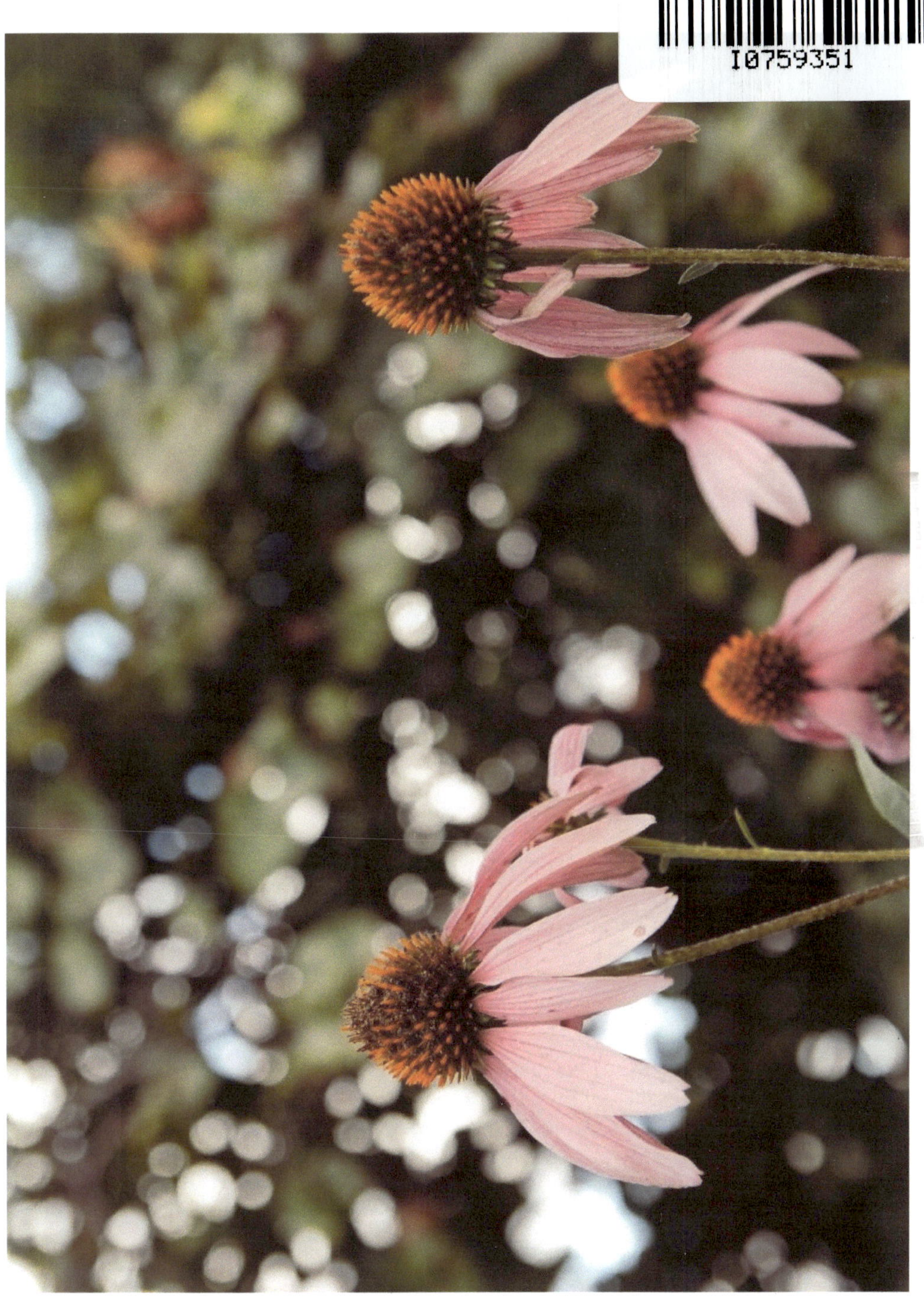

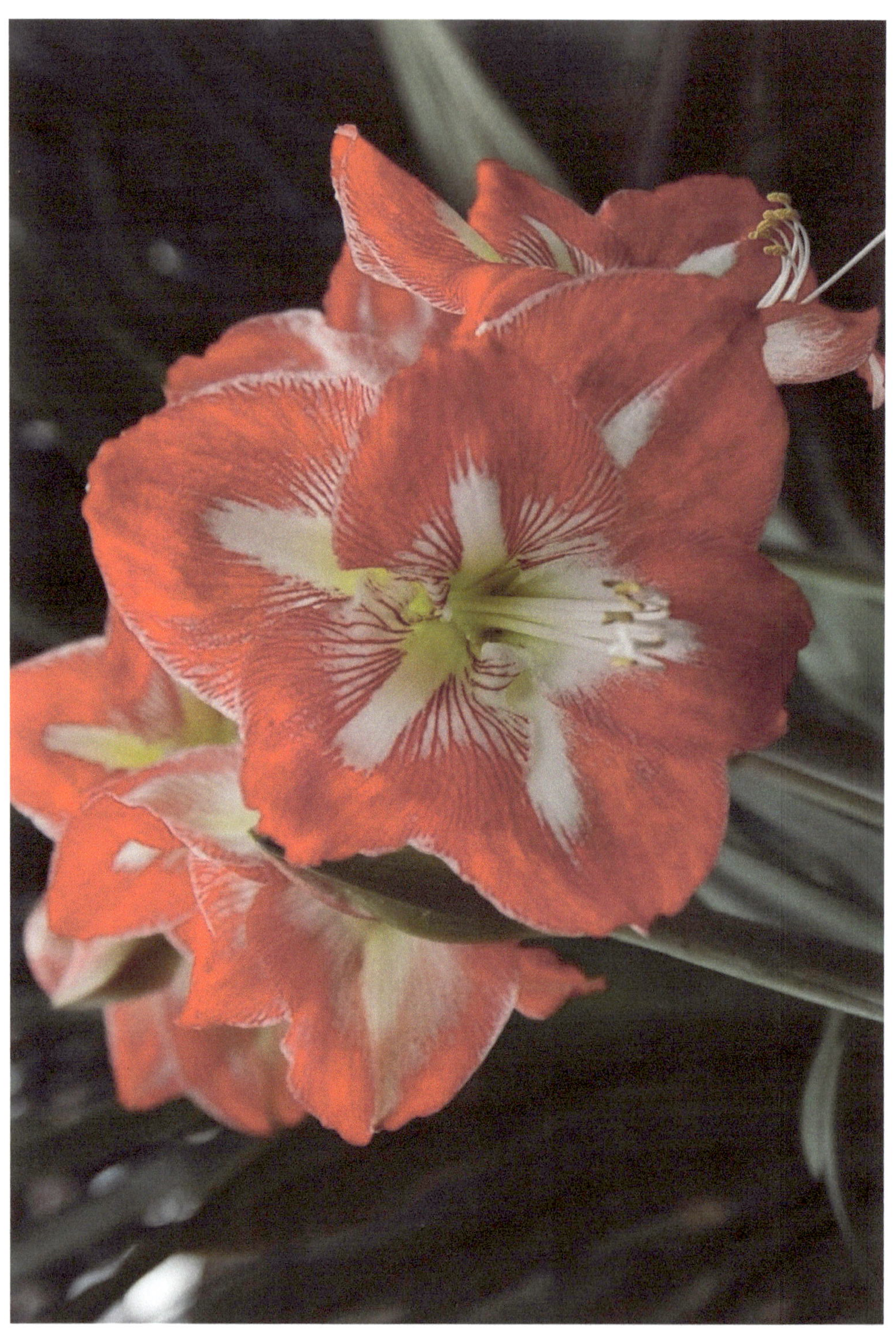

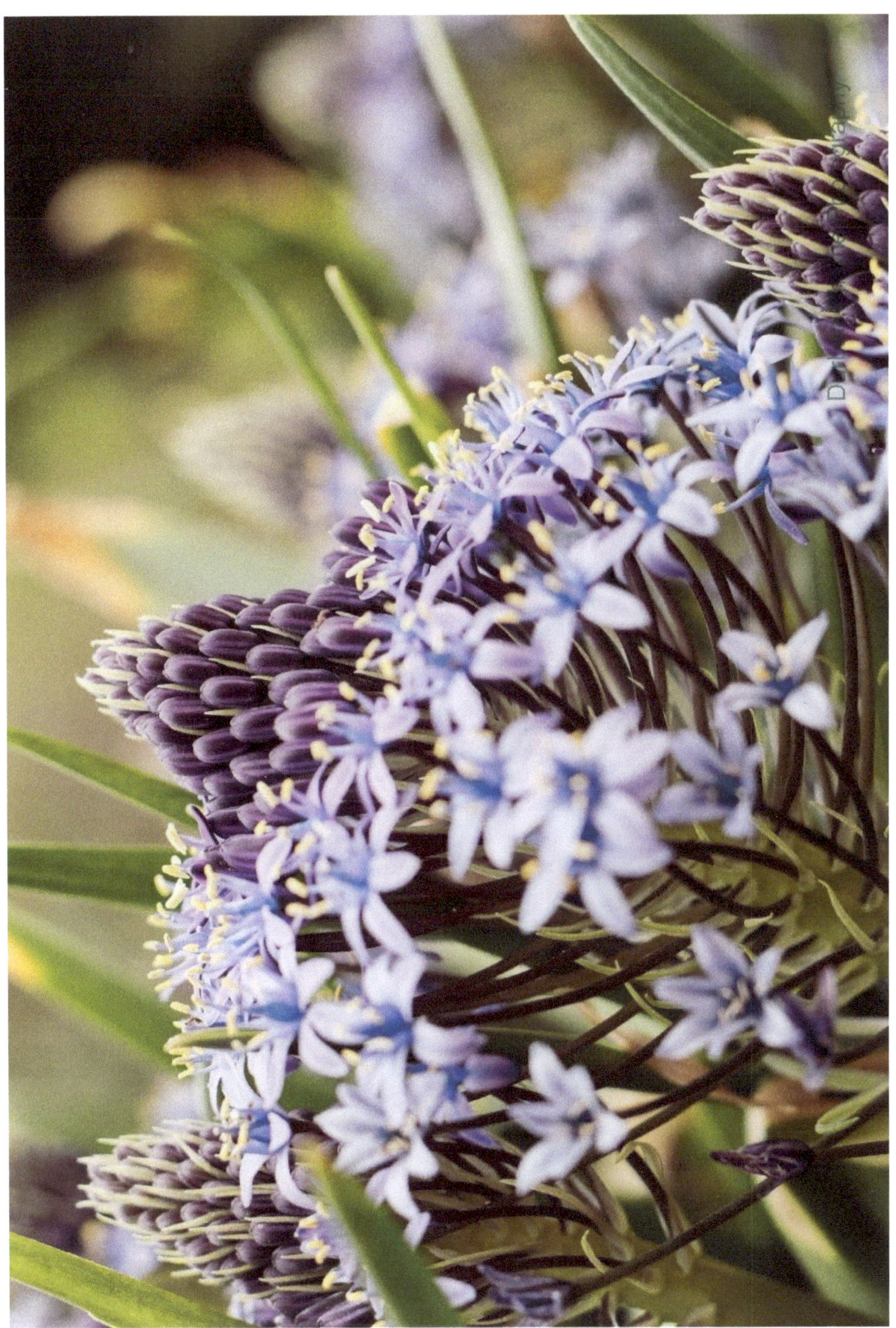

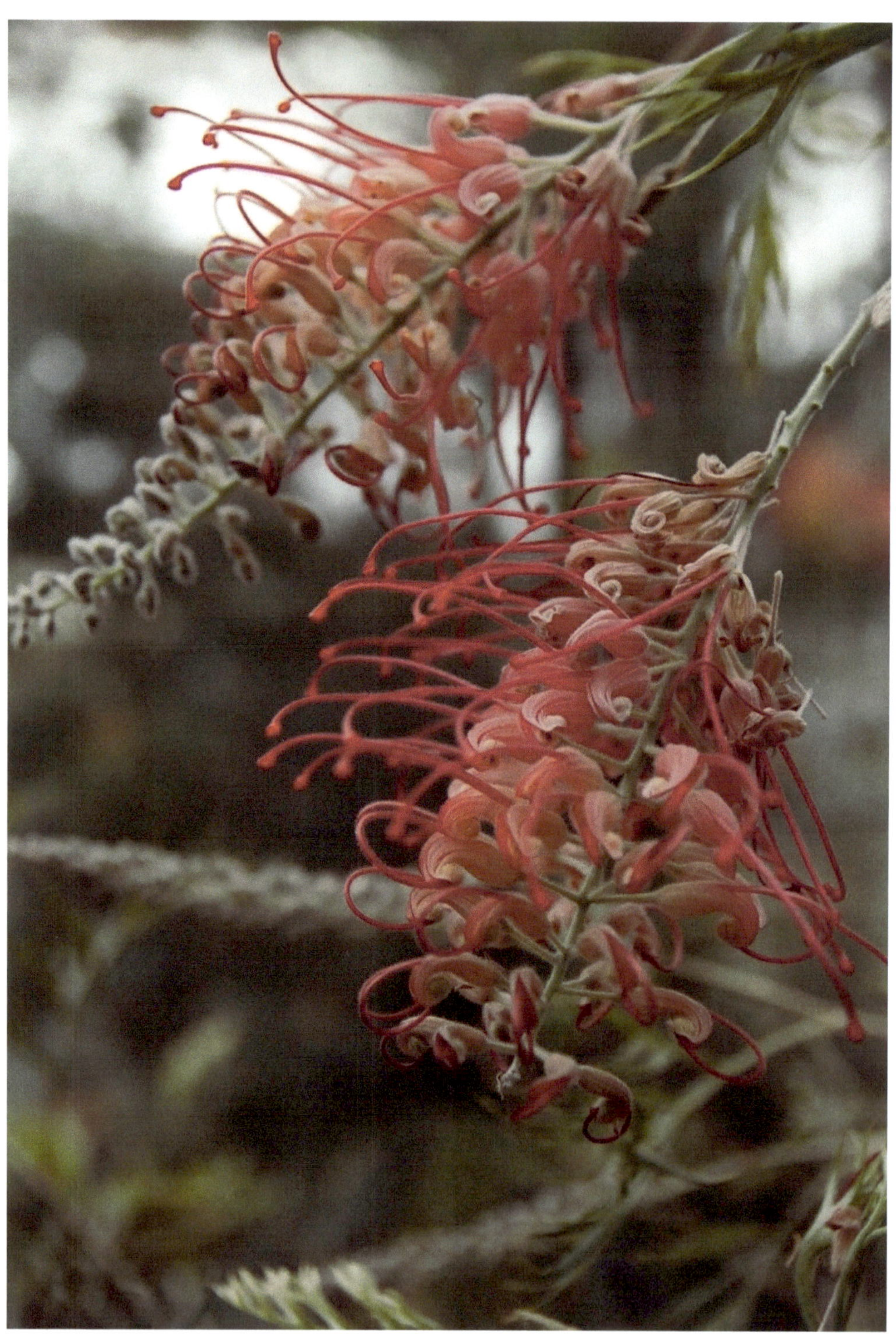

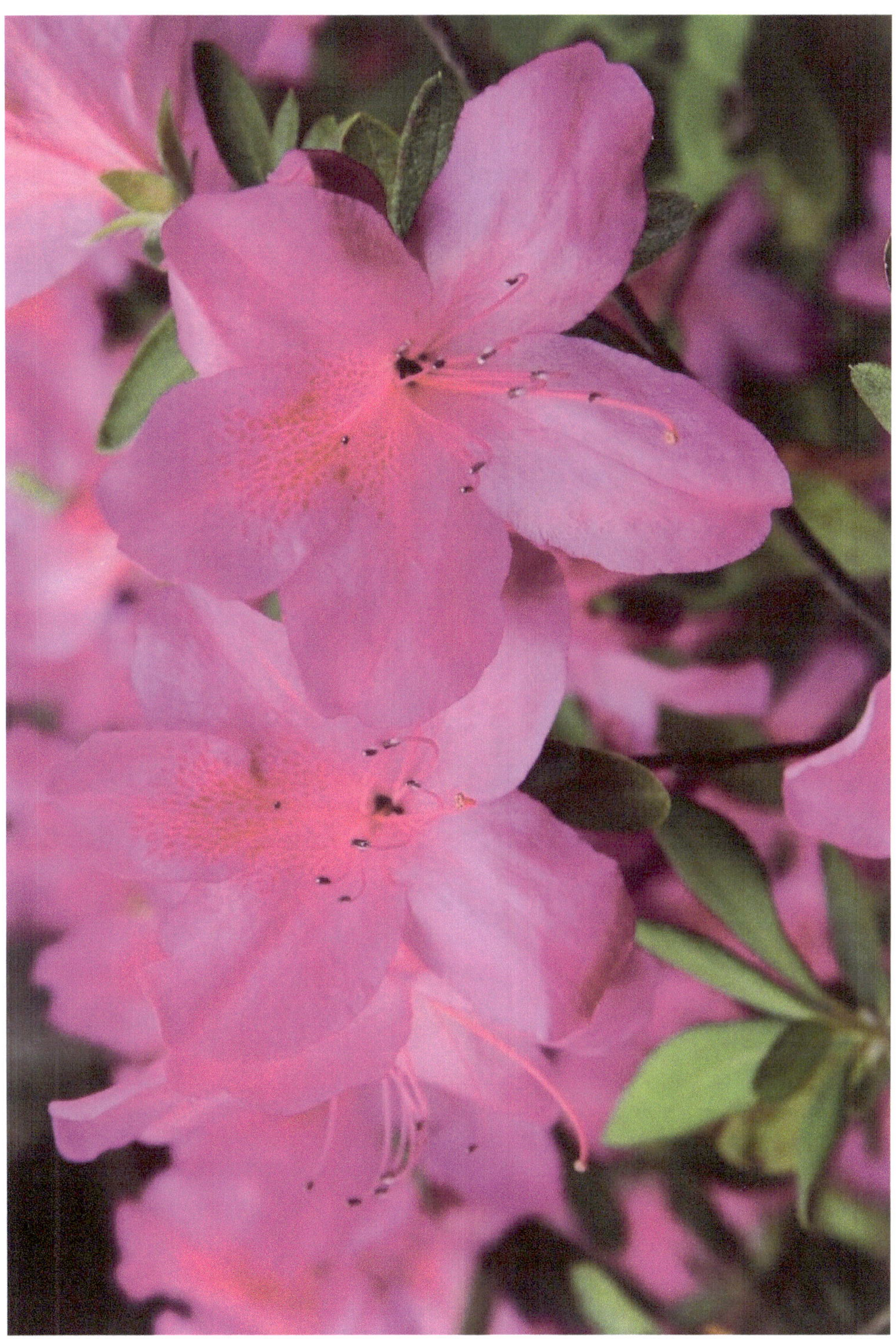

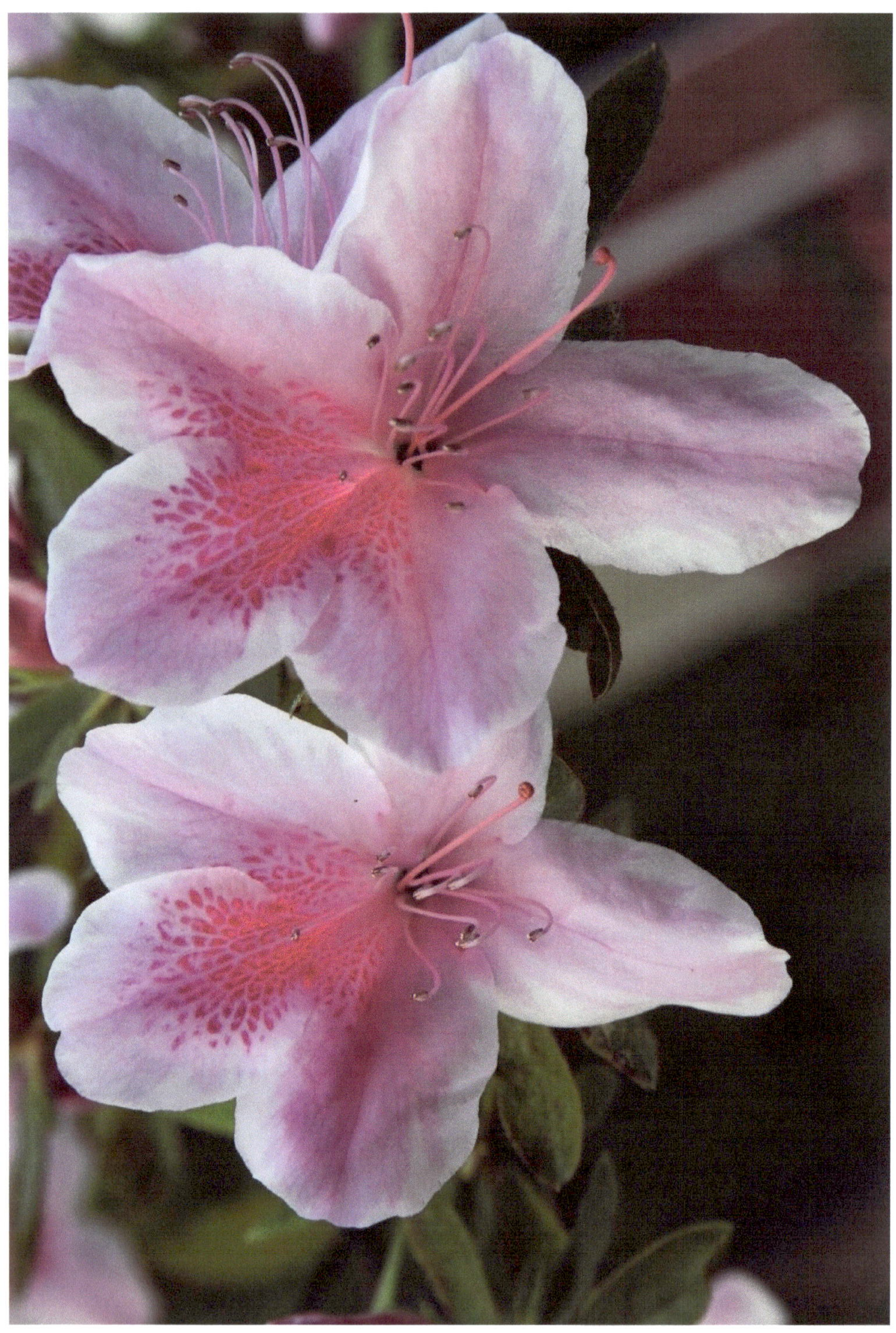

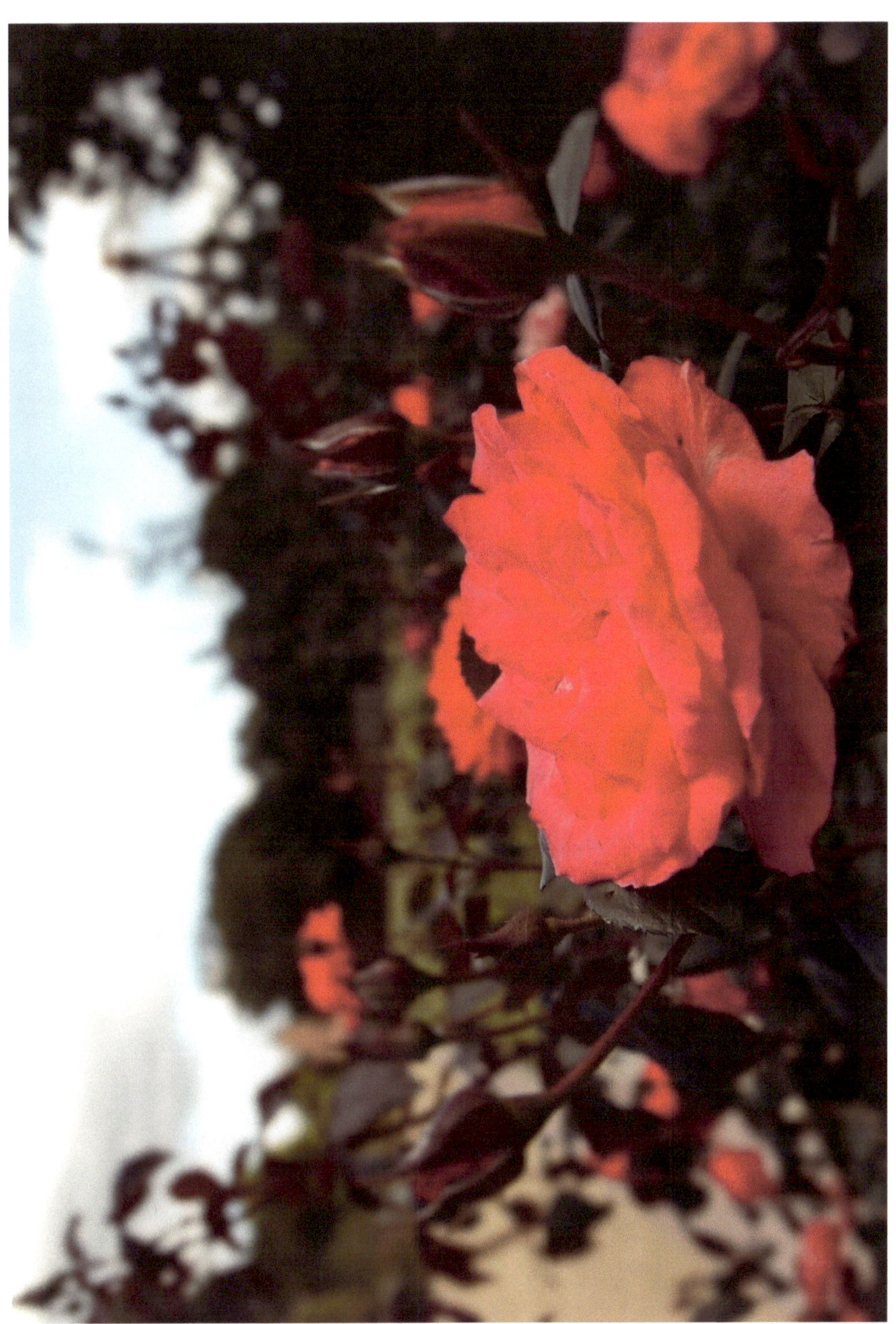

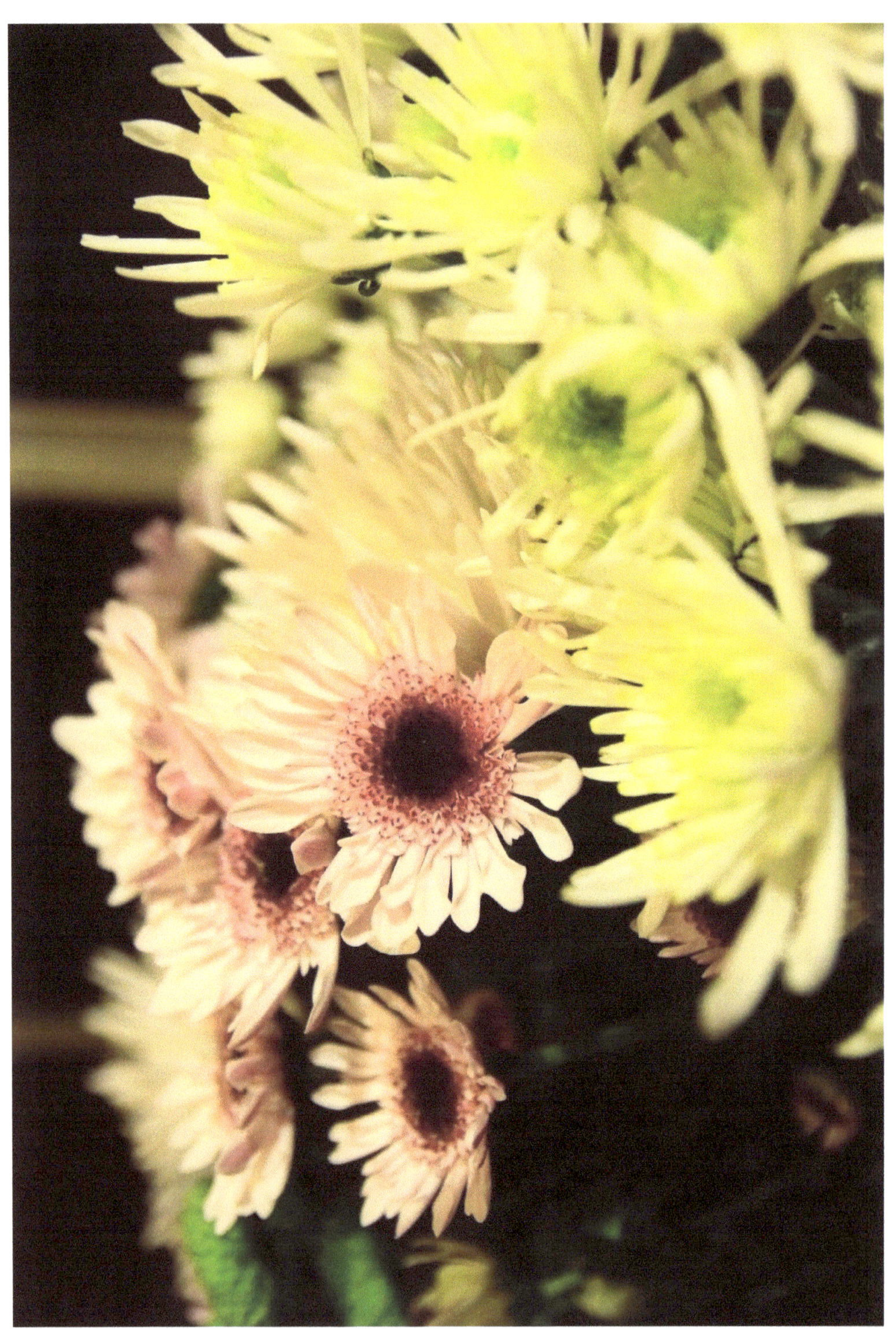

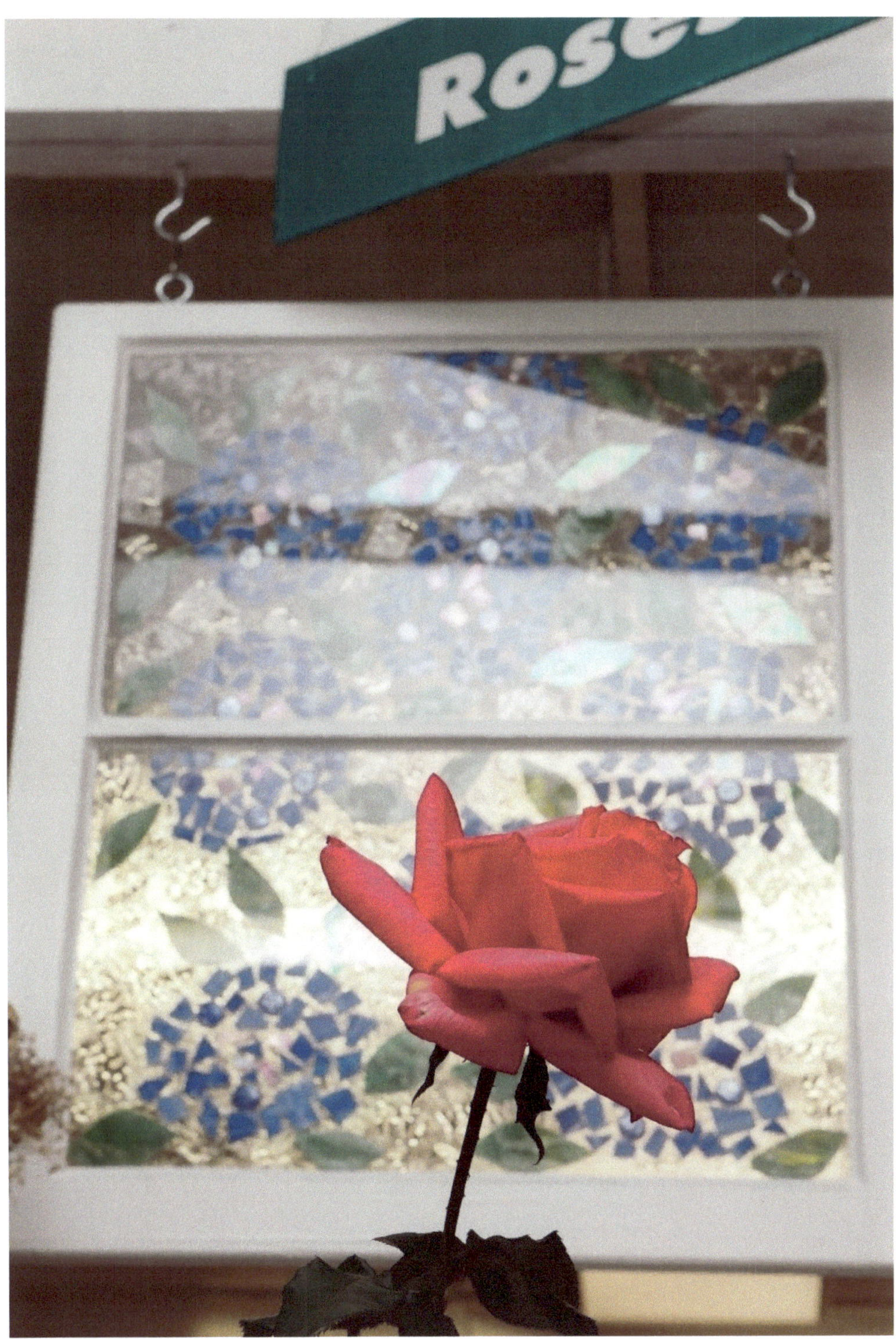
Roses

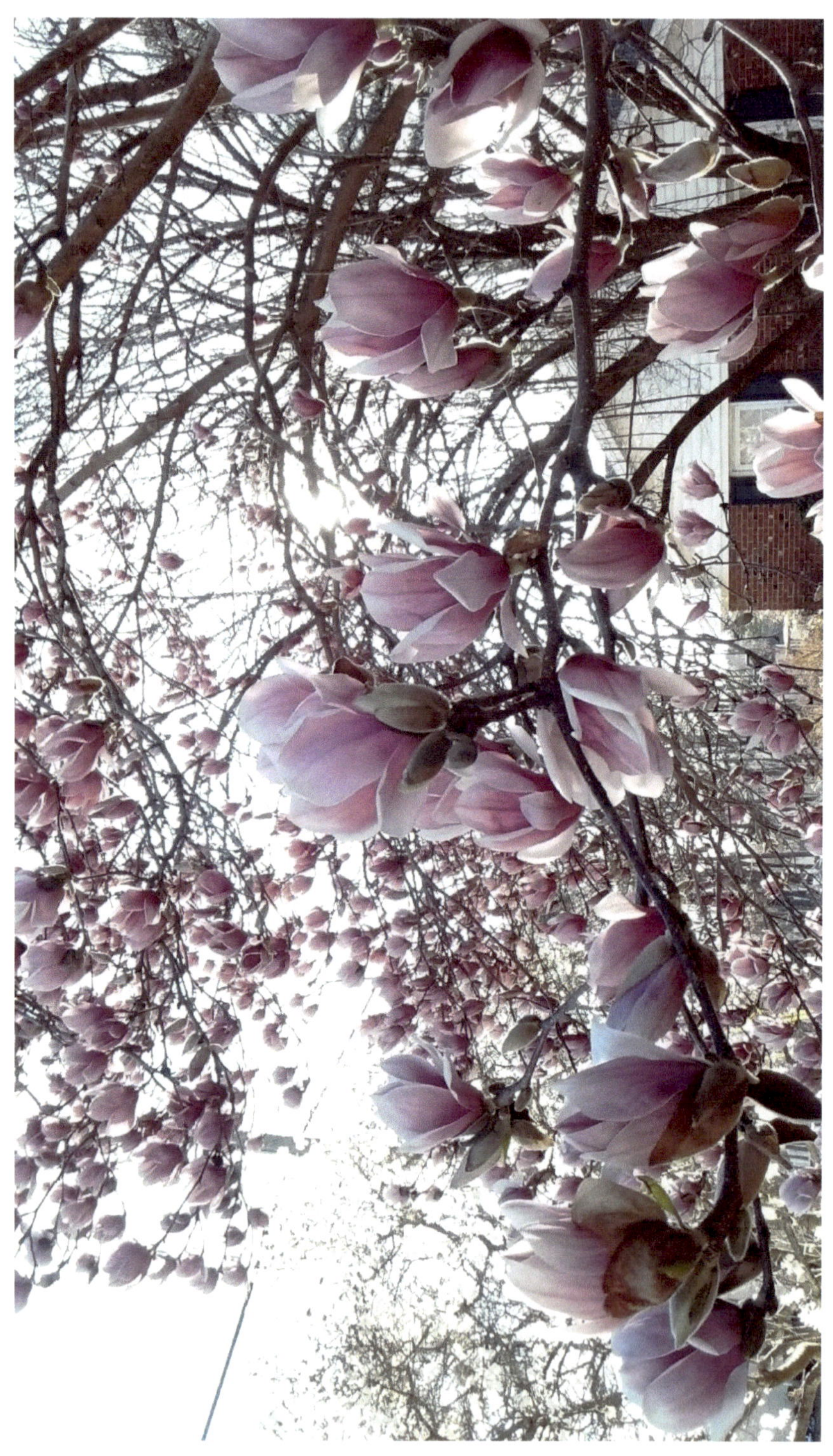

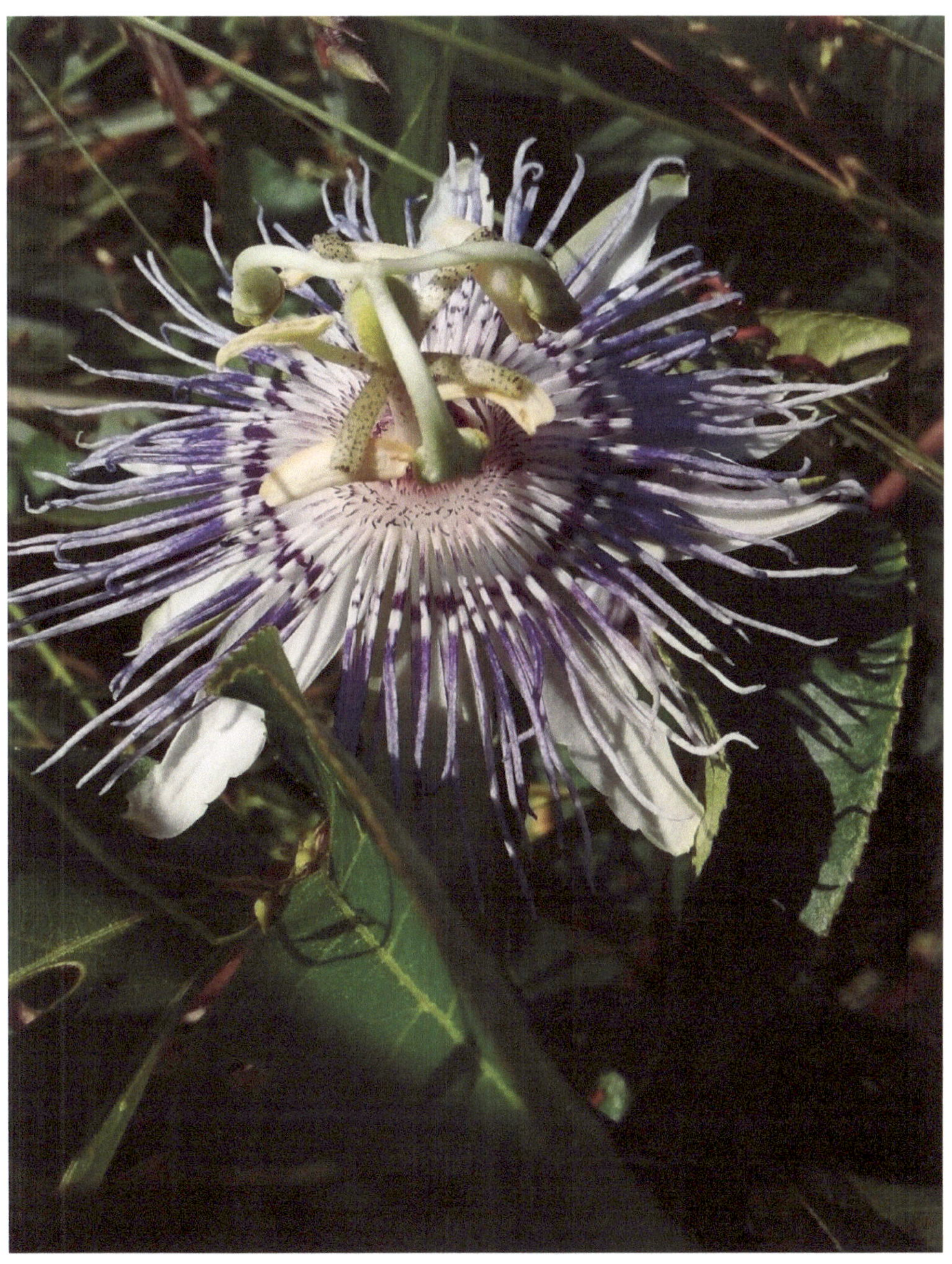

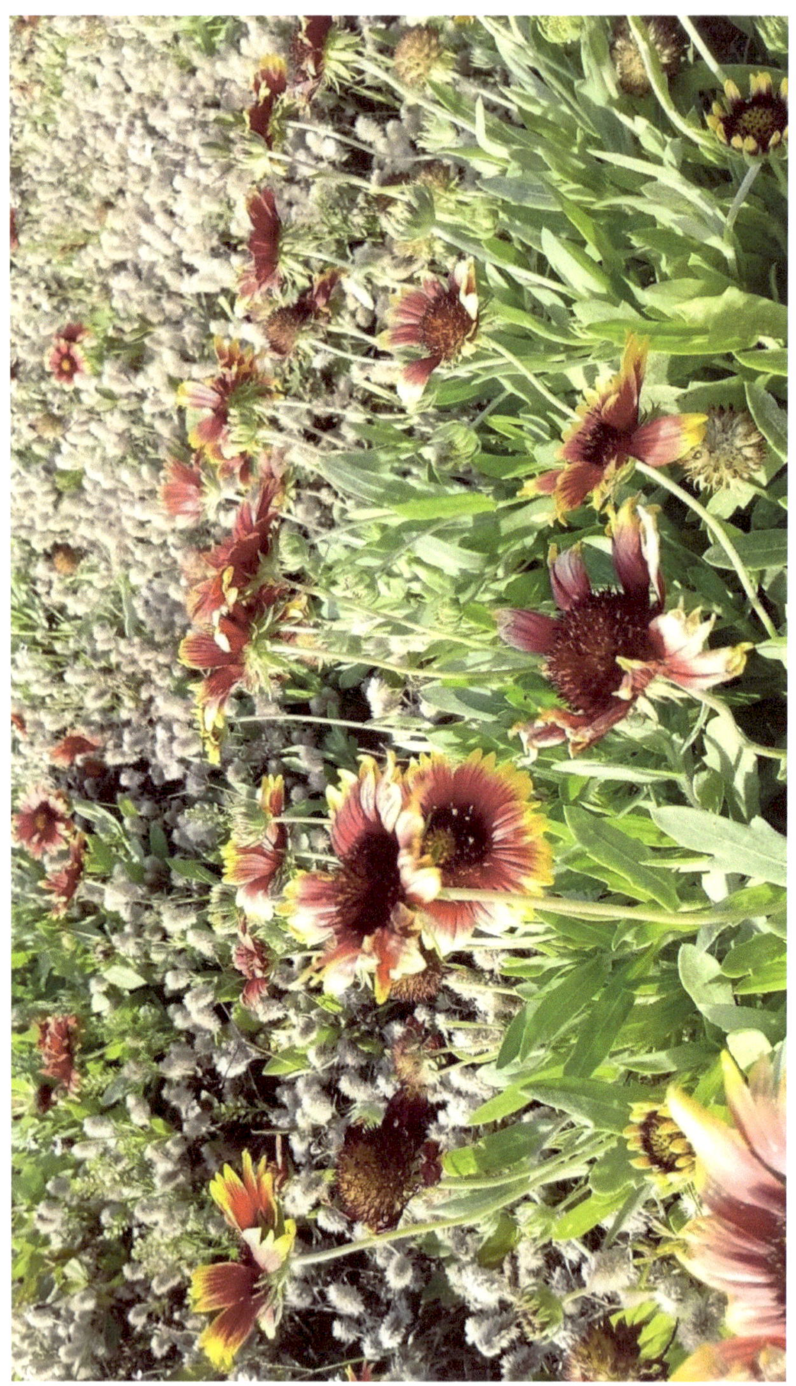

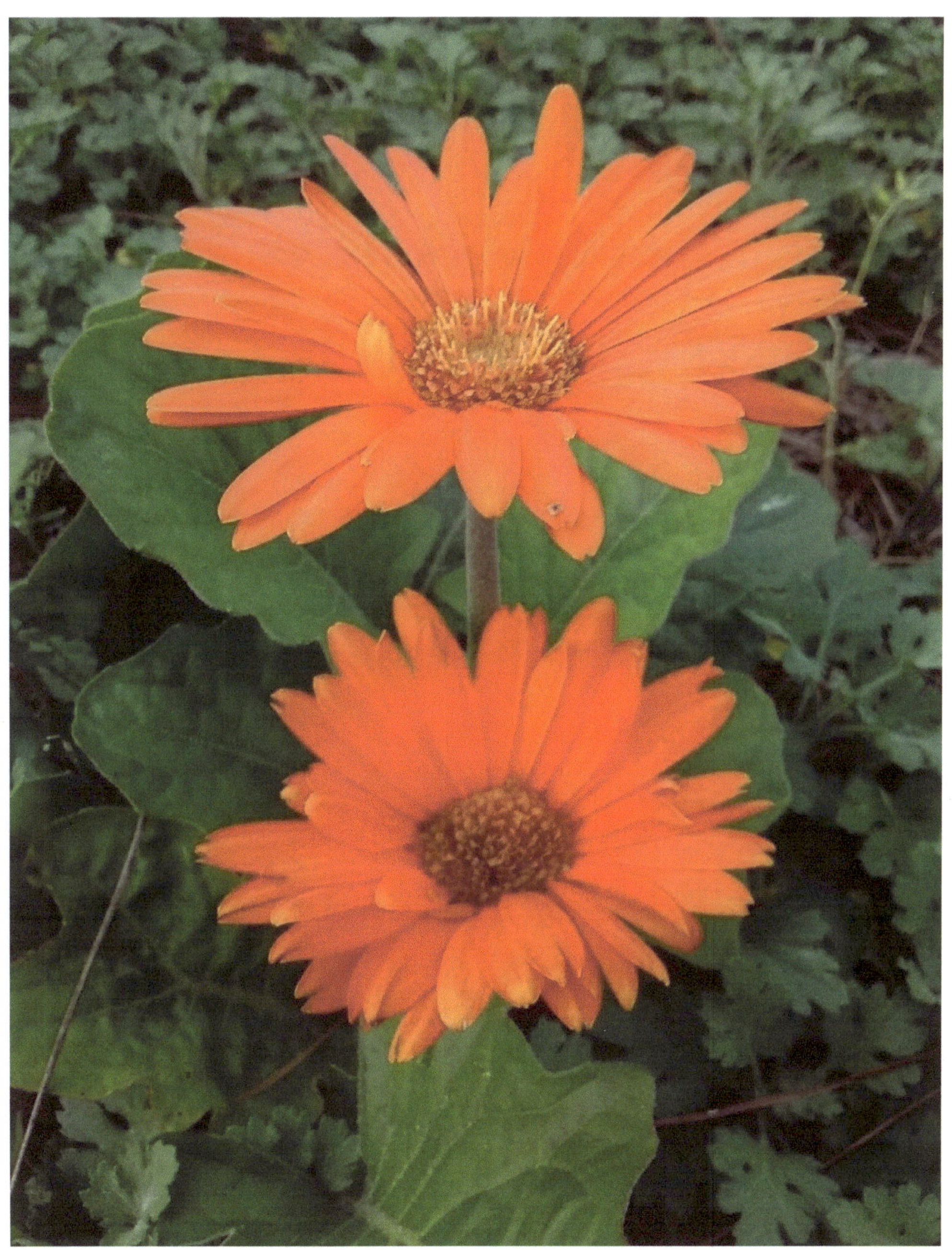

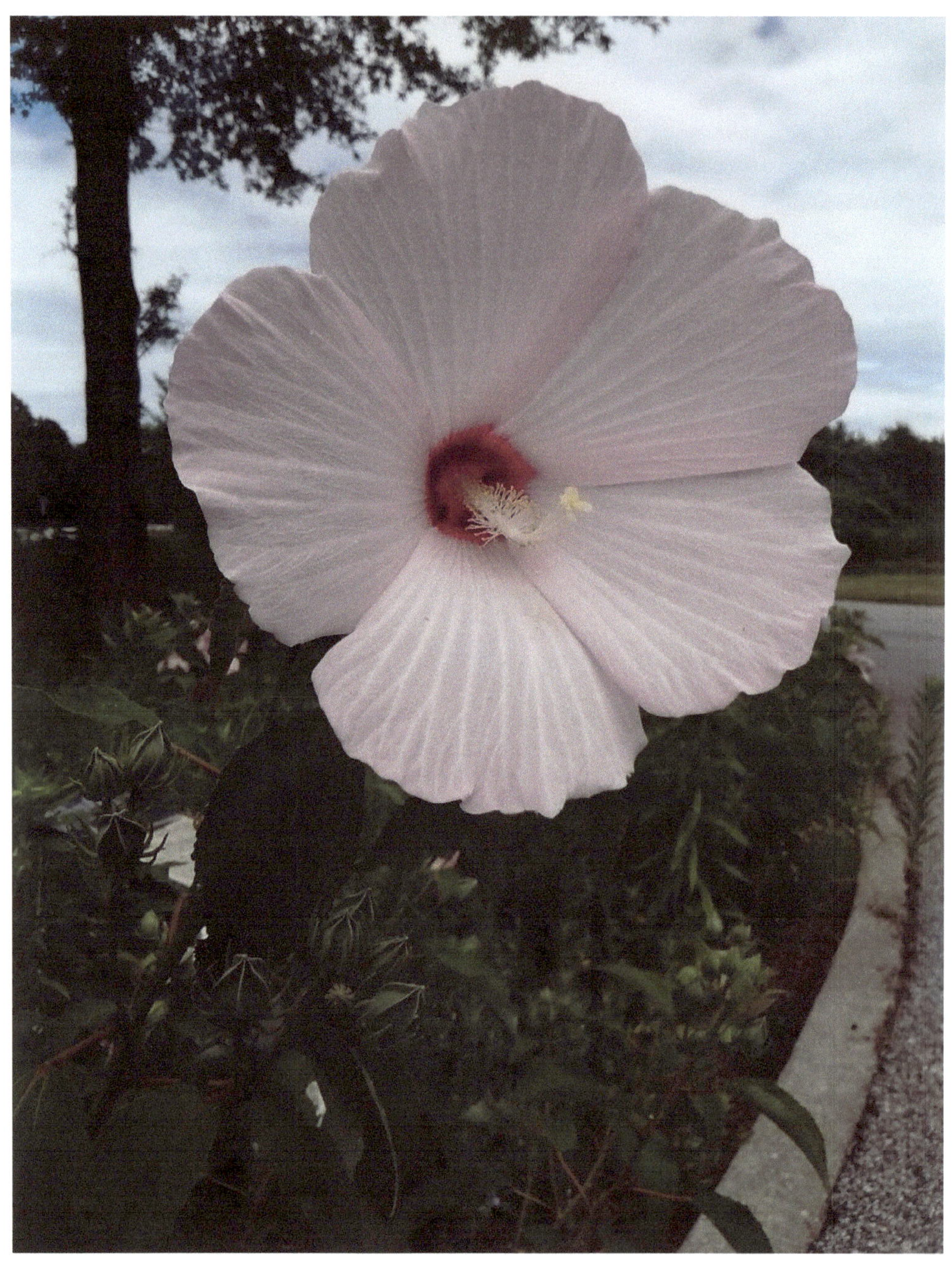

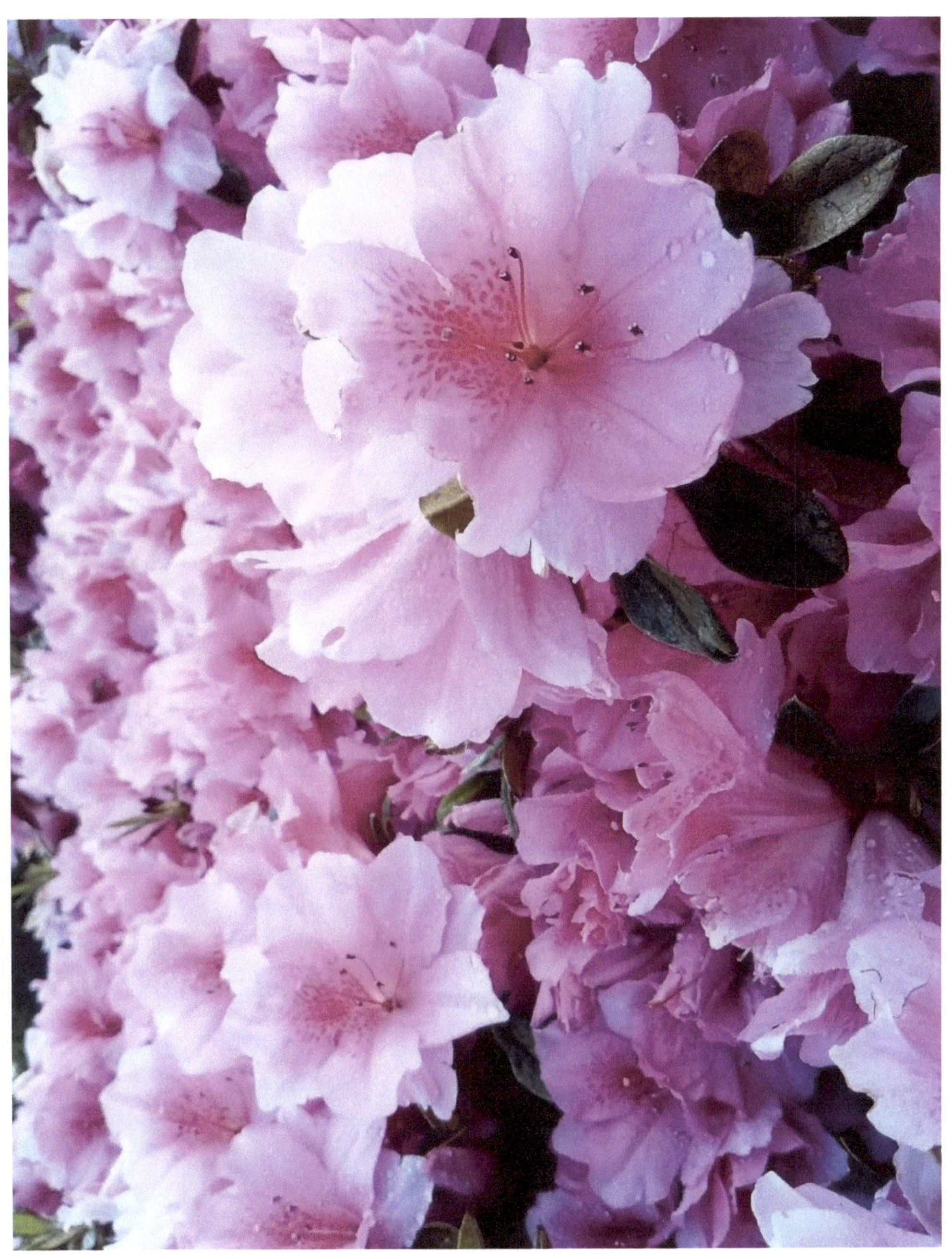

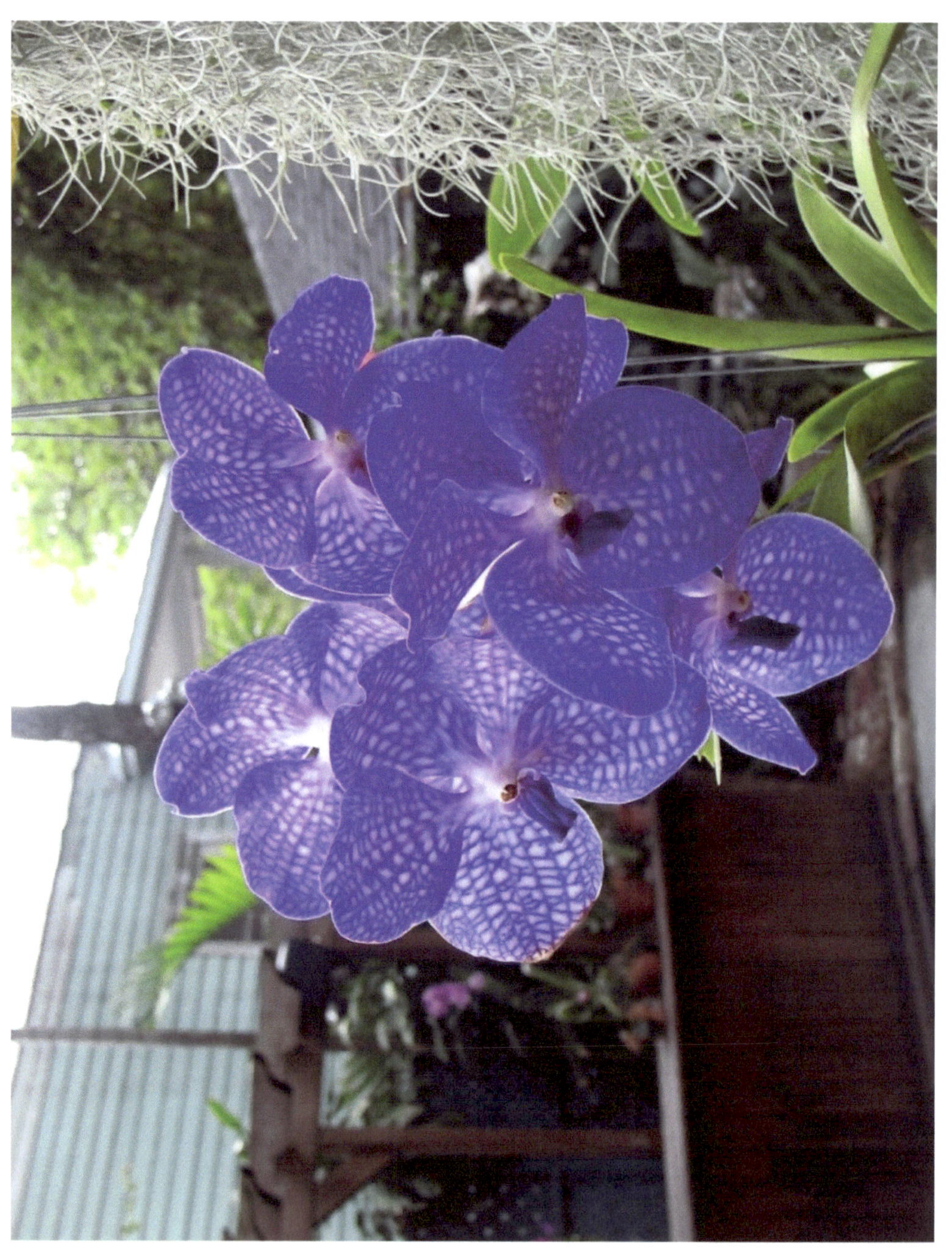

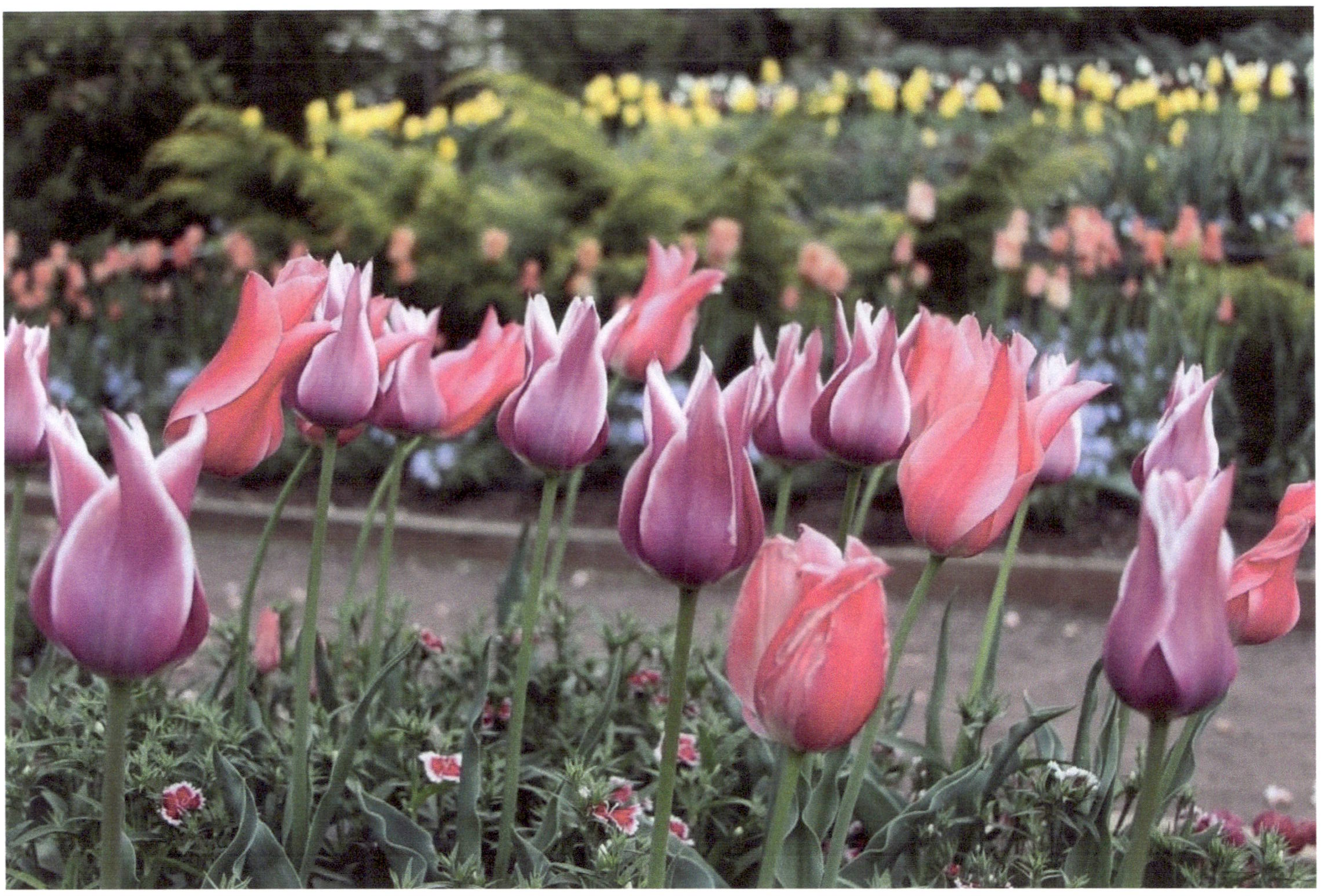

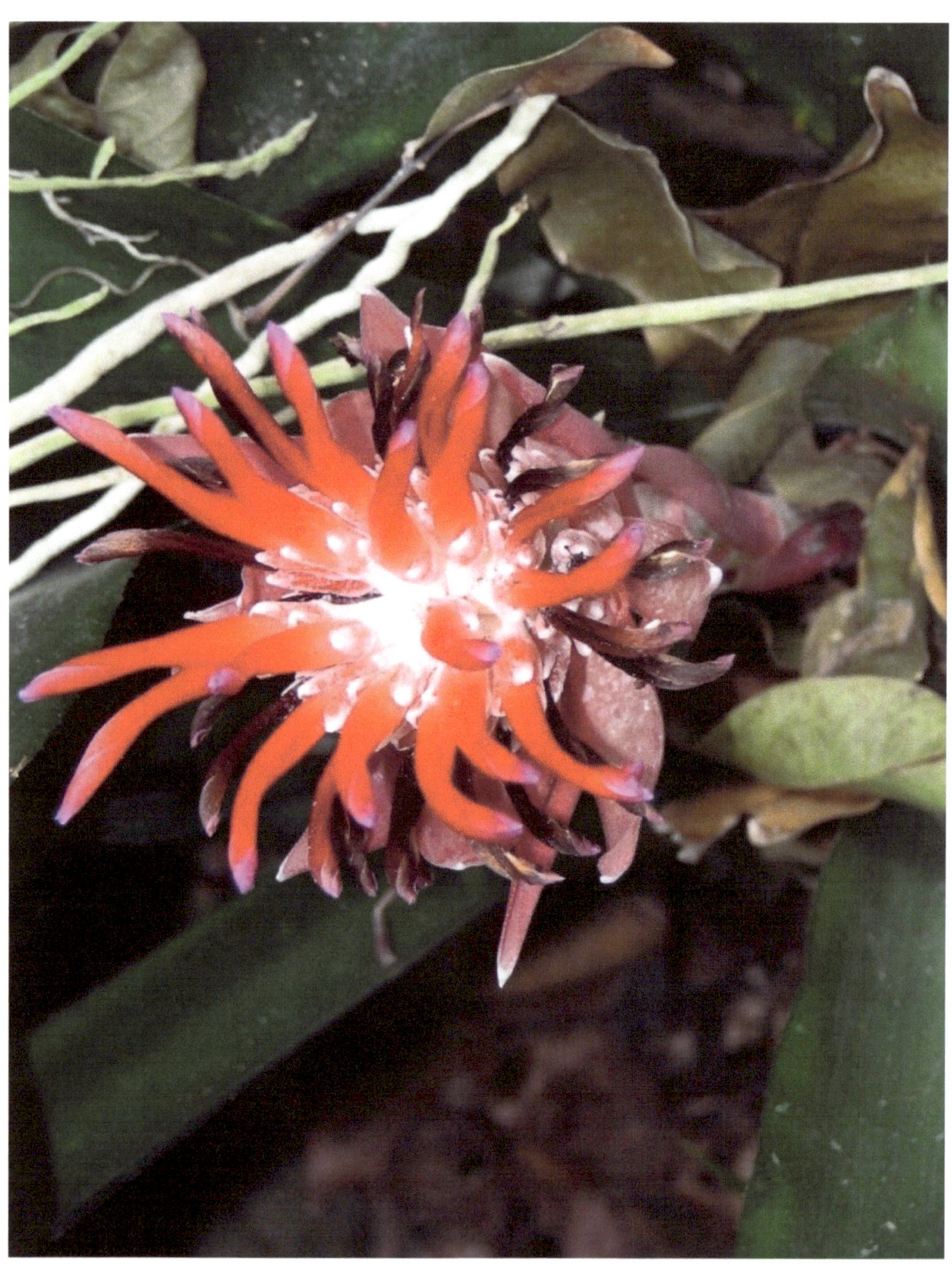

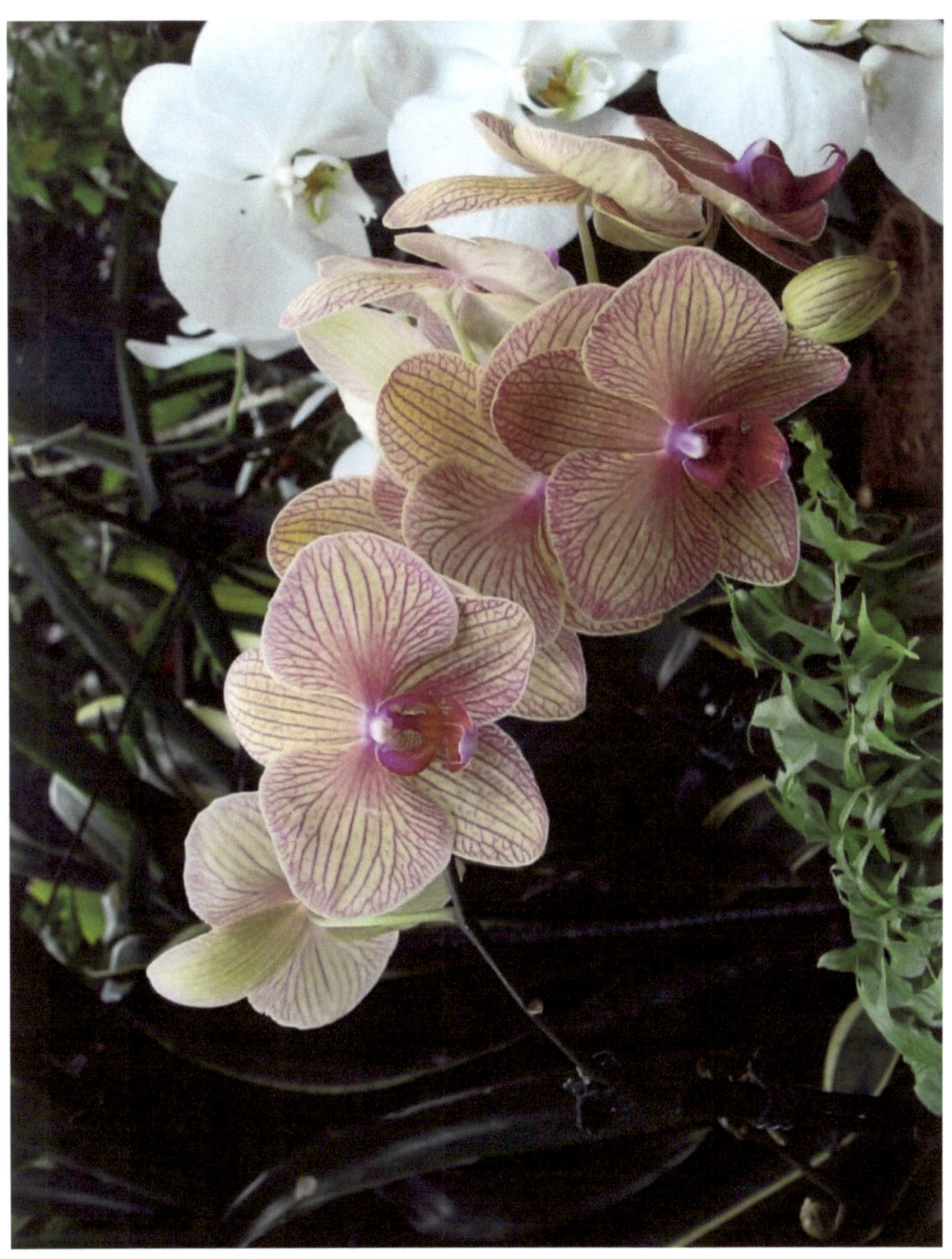

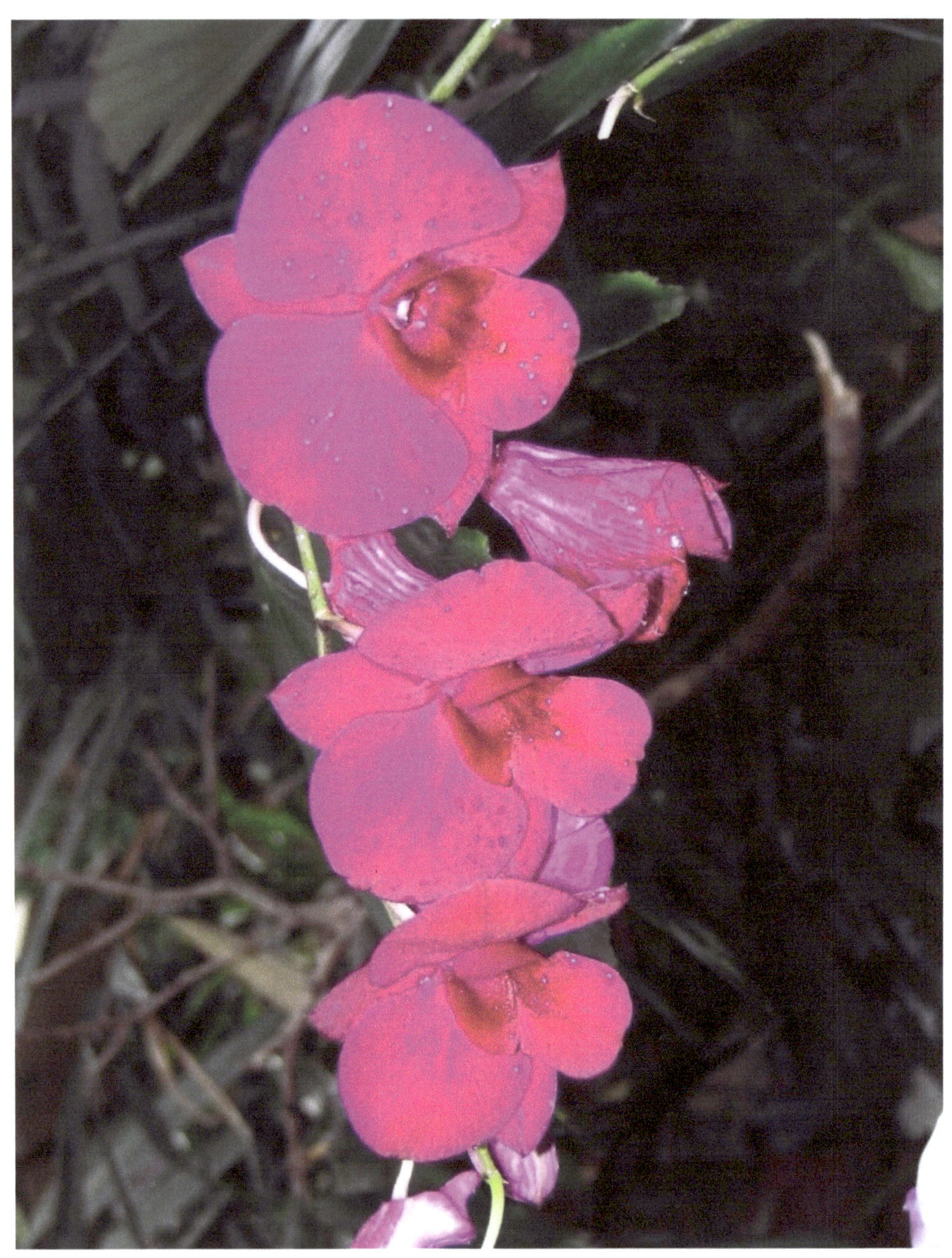

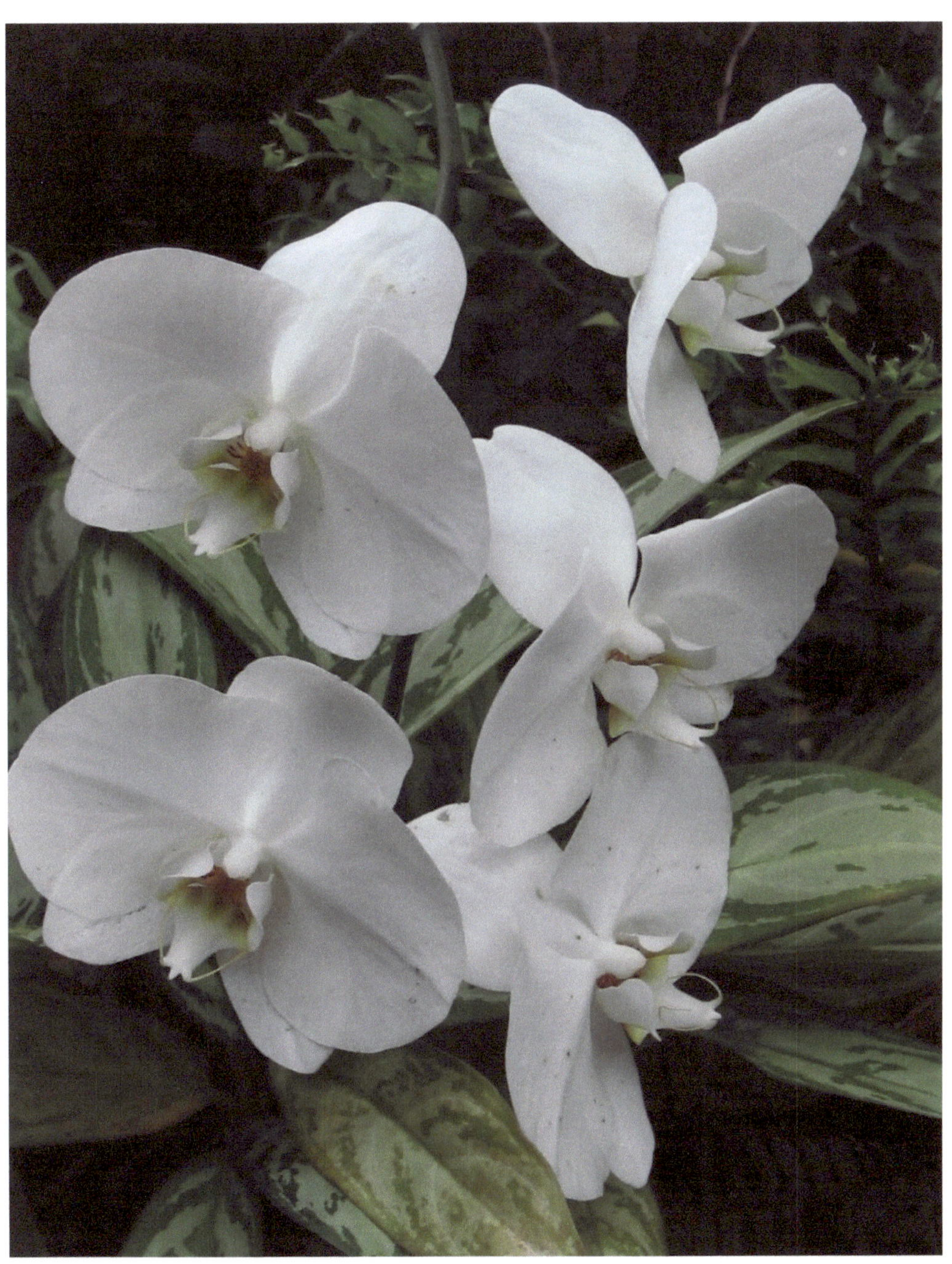

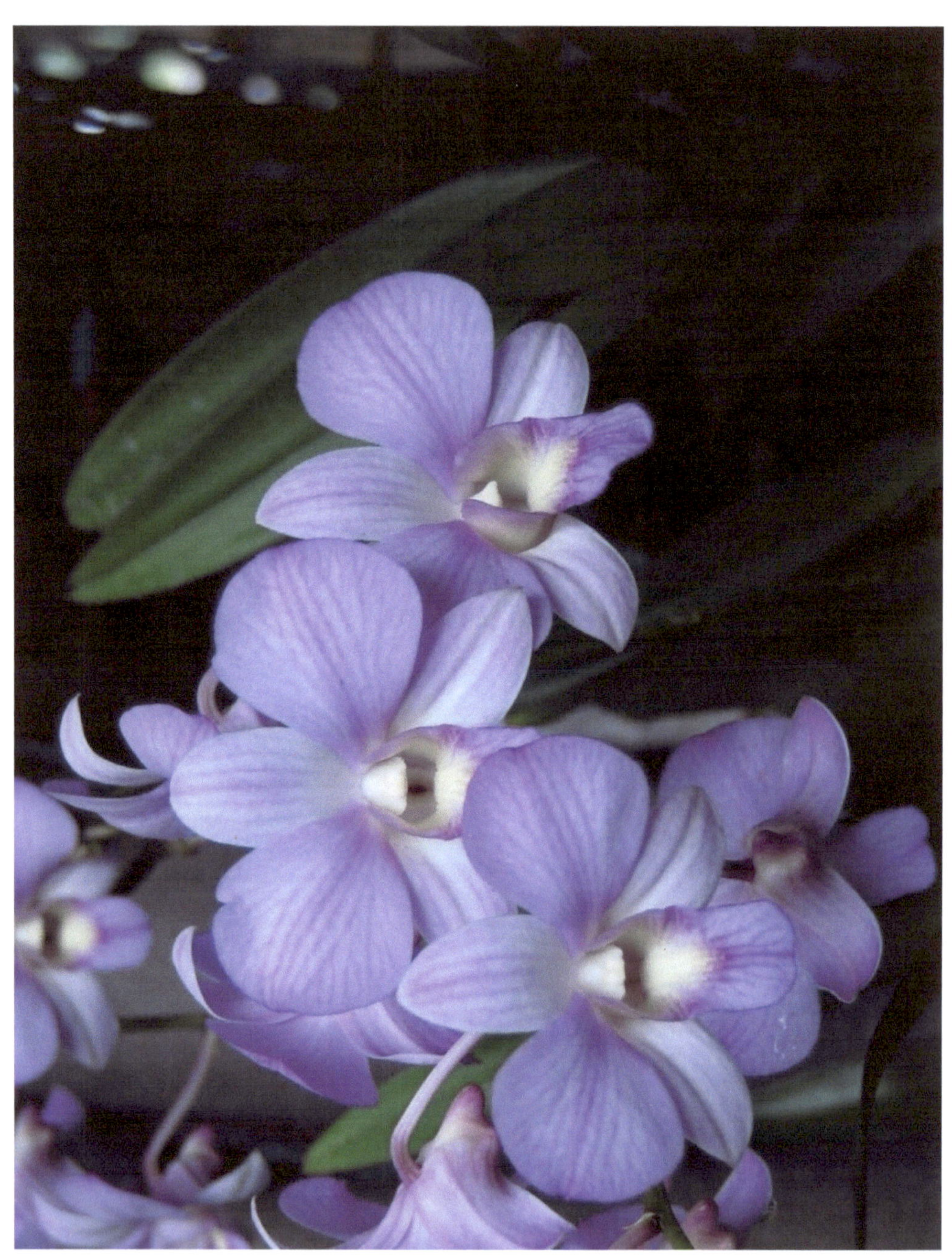

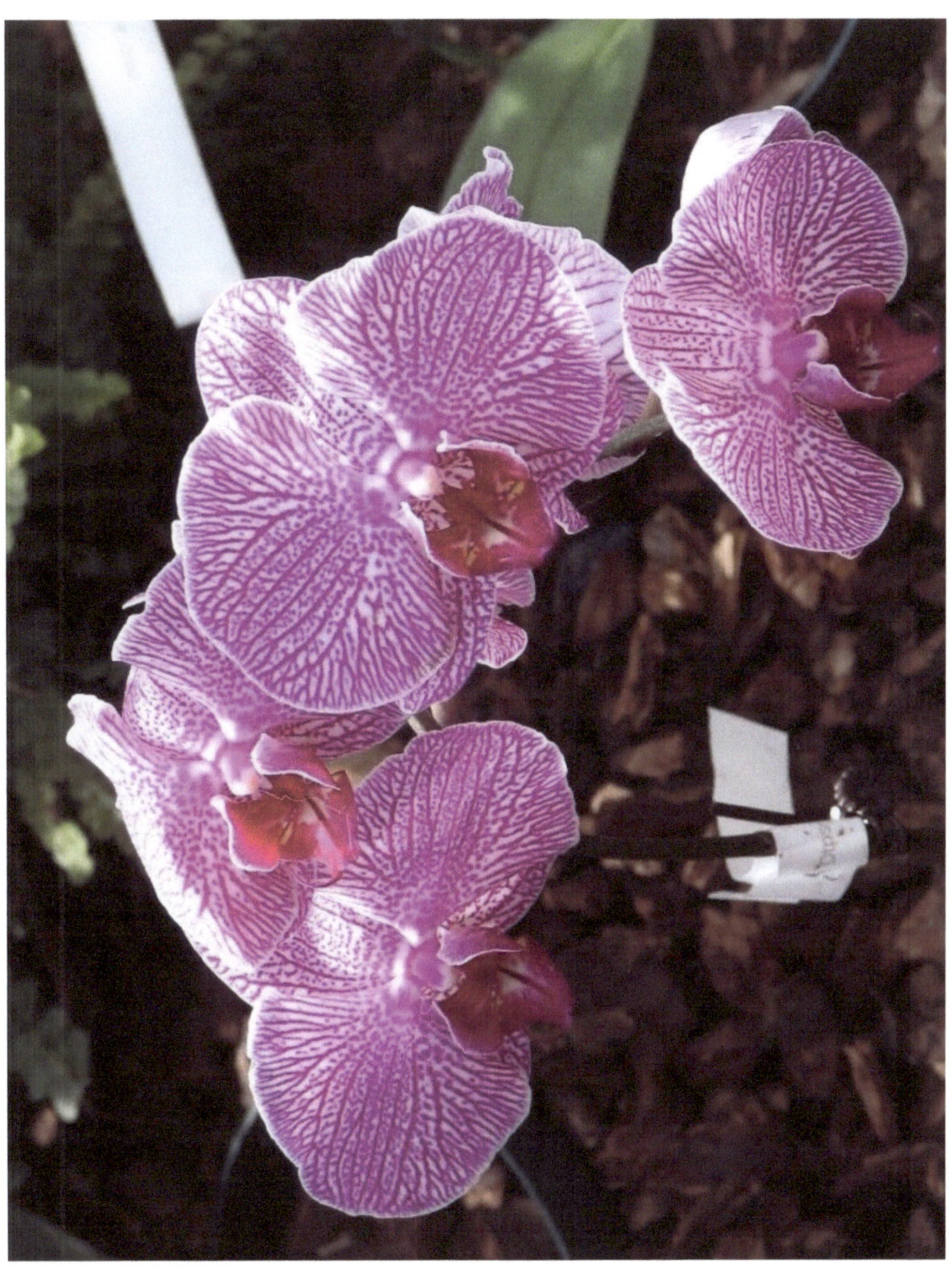

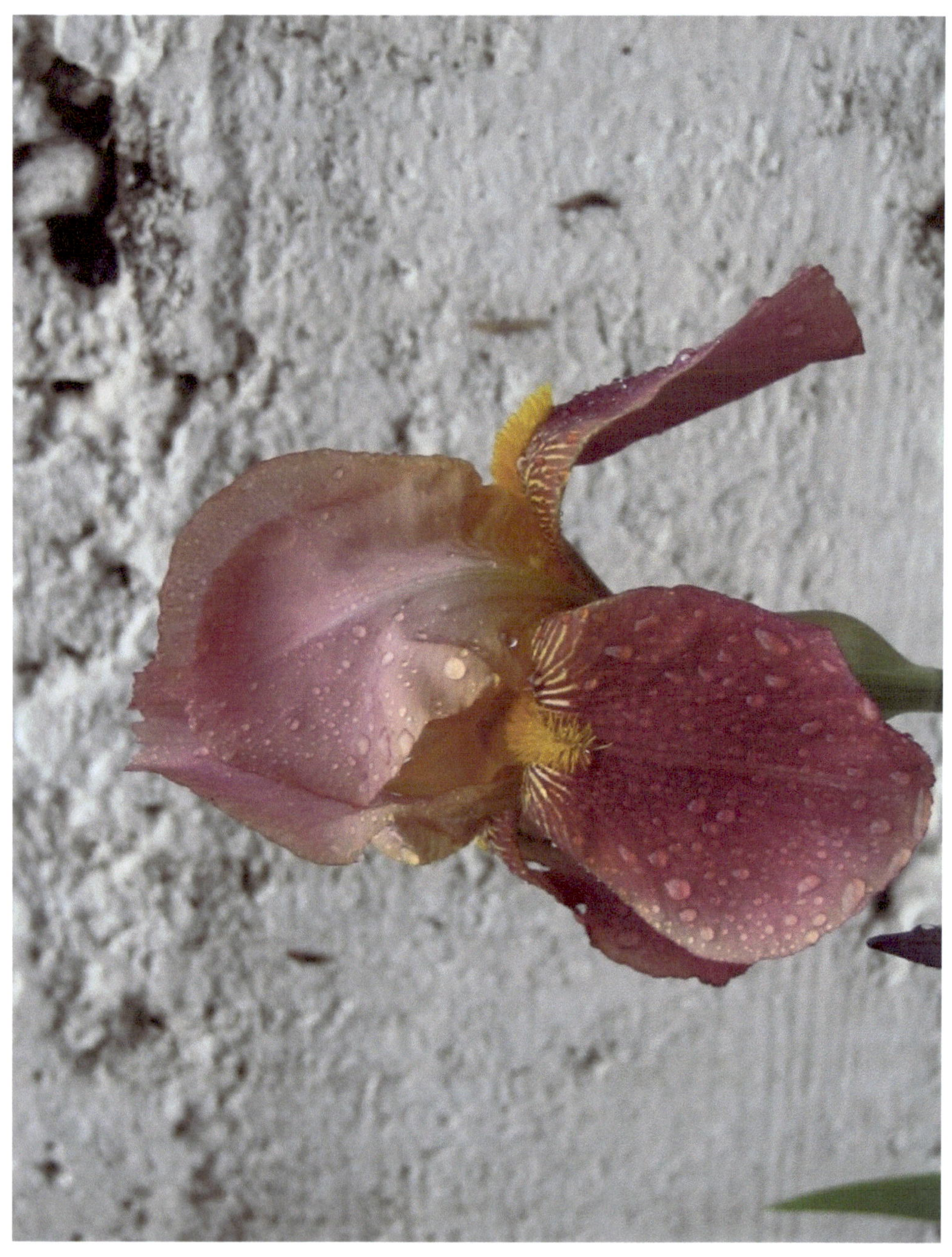

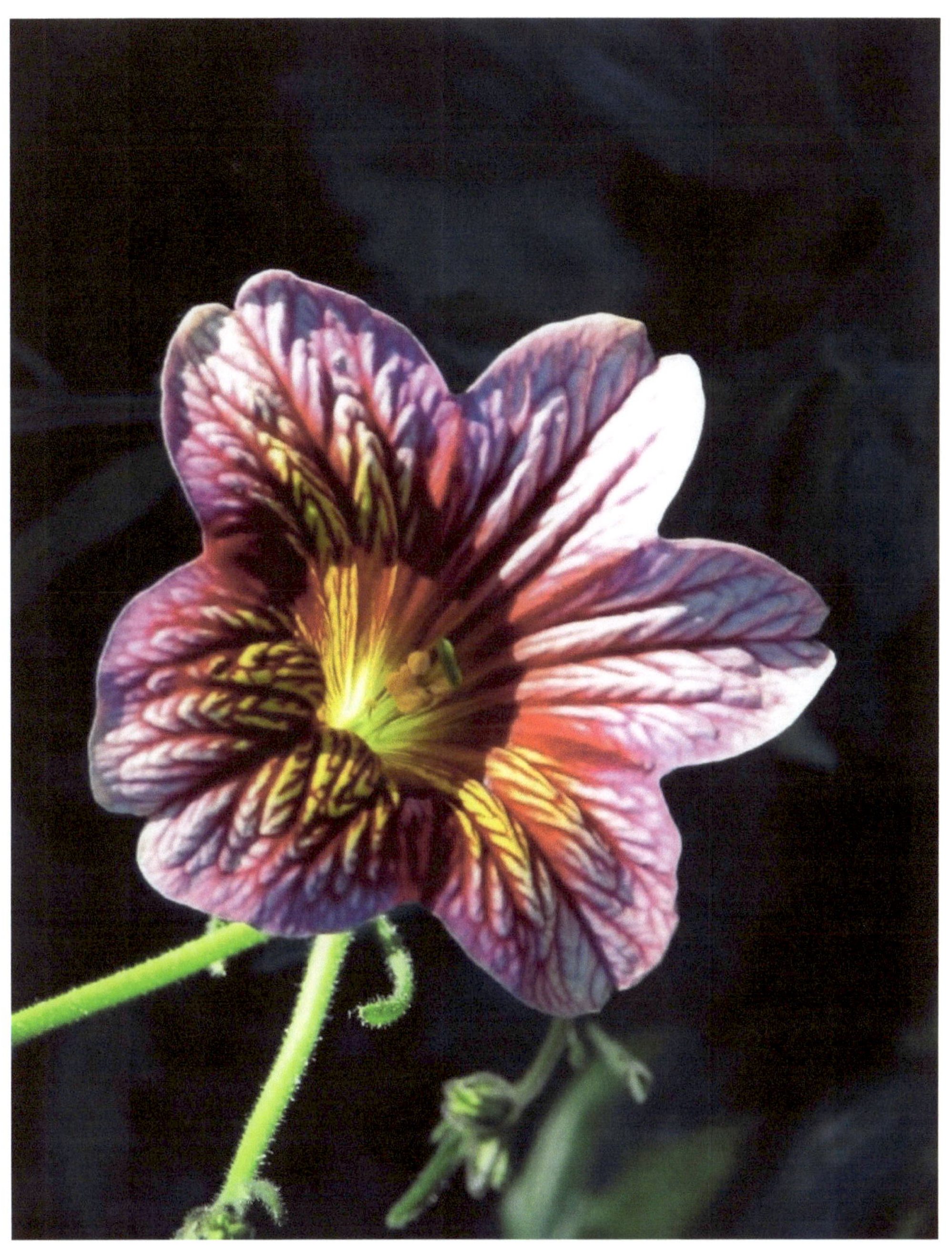

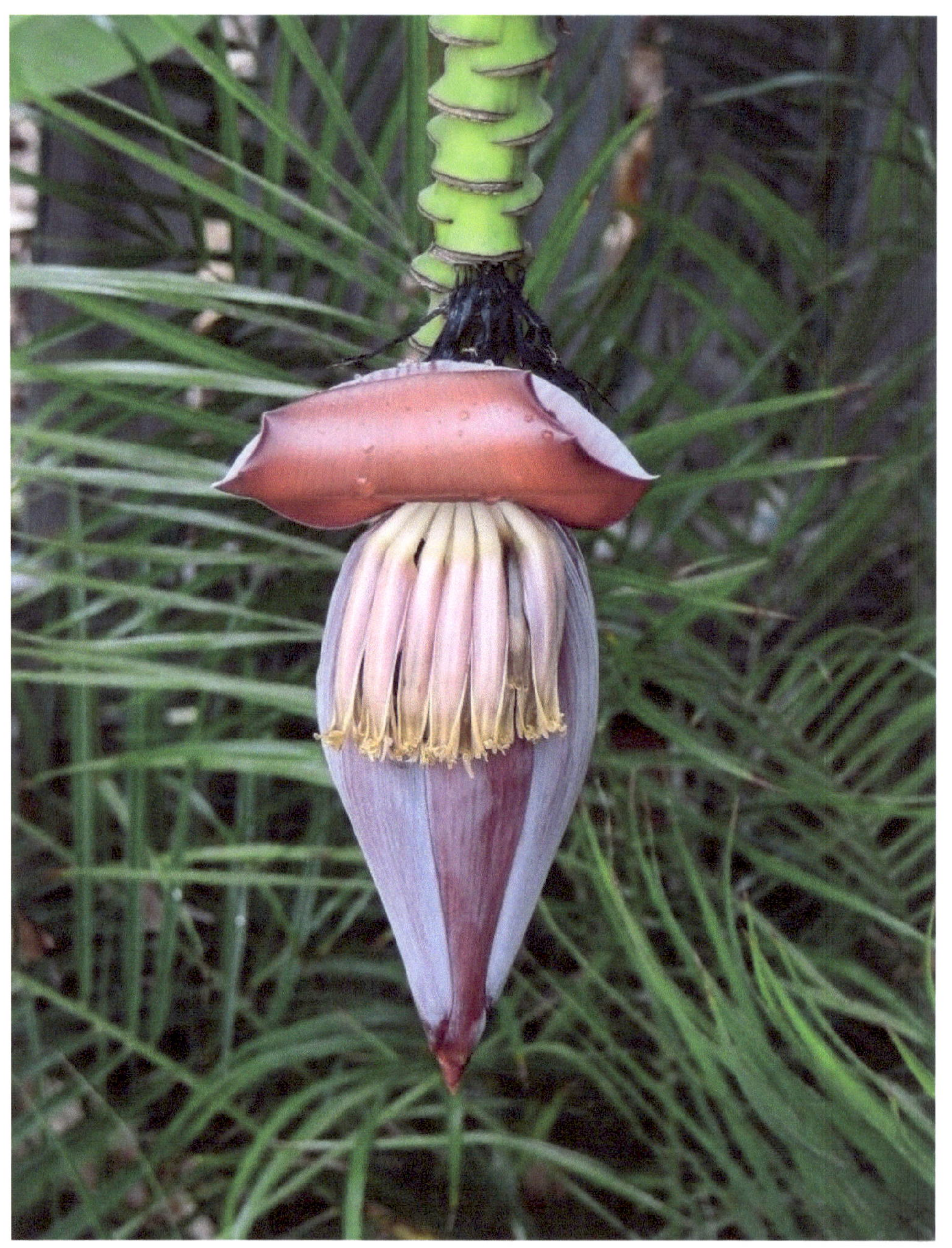

Check out my other books avaiable.

CREATIVE CAKES

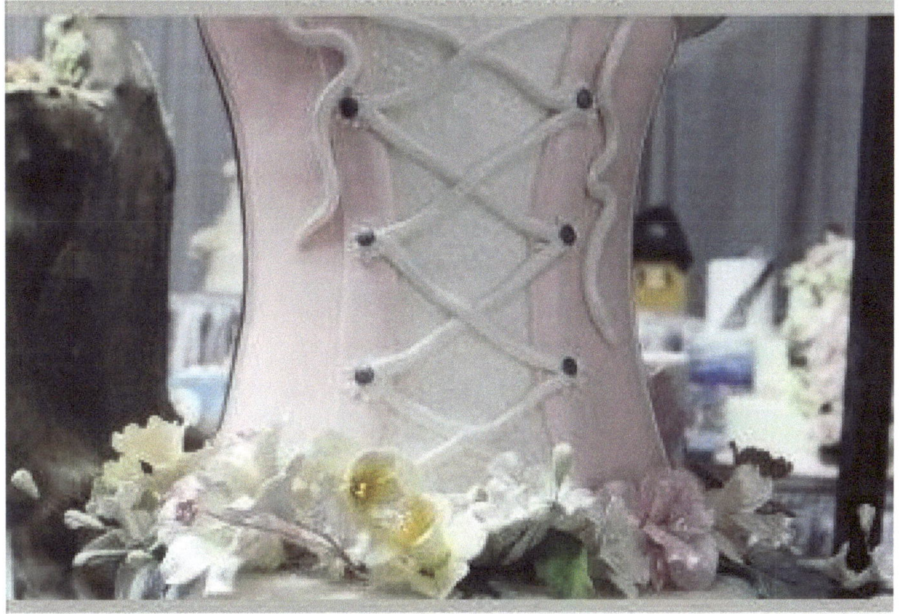

BEAUTIFUL CAKES

MISC RAMBLING

The end.

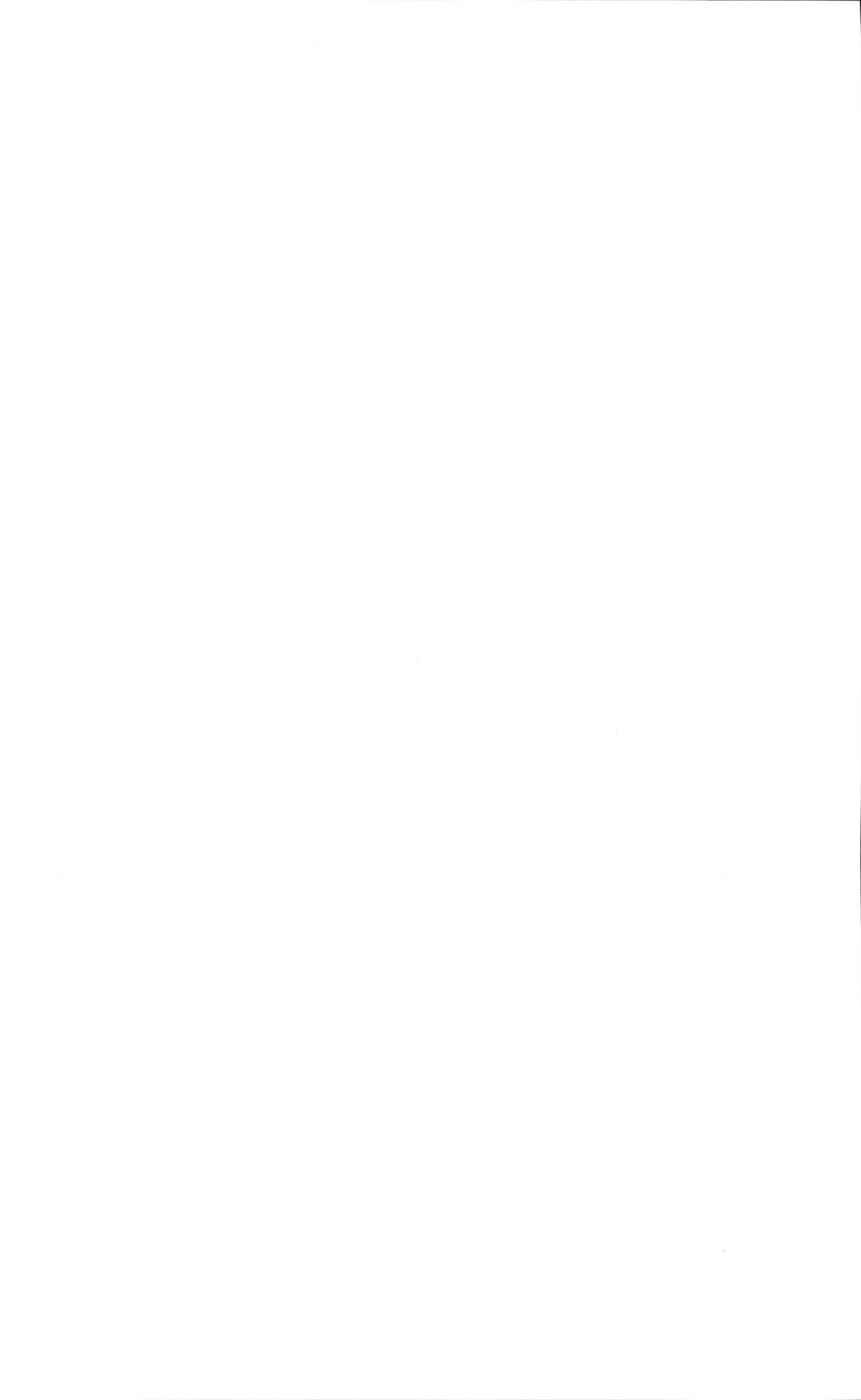